Breath, Suspended

poems by

Diane Alters

Finishing Line Press
Georgetown, Kentucky

Breath, Suspended

Copyright © 2022 by Diane Alters
ISBN 978-1-64662-797-4 First Edition
All rights reserved under International and Pan-American Copyright Conventions. No part of this book may be reproduced in any manner whatsoever without written permission from the publisher, except in the case of brief quotations embodied in critical articles and reviews.

ACKNOWLEDGMENTS

Thank you to editors of the journals and magazines in which the following poems have appeared:

Calyx Journal: "This Face" and "In Lima: Small Boxes," which appears here as "Small Boxes"
Crosswinds Poetry Journal: "Pools Form," which appears here as "Water in an Eye"
Pilgrimage Magazine: "Lost"

The two paintings described in "Small Boxes" were in the Museo de Arte Contemporáneo: *La ejecución de Túpac Amaru* by Fernando De Szyszlo and *Caja negra* by Alfredo Márquez and Ángel Valdez. The Vallejo poem referenced in "Water in an Eye" is "Los heraldos negros" and in "Sidewalk Pieces," "A mi hermano Miguel."

Publisher: Leah Huete de Maines
Editor: Christen Kincaid
Cover Art: Diane Alters
Author Photo: Stacy J. Platt
Cover Design: HR Hegnauer

Order online: www.finishinglinepress.com
also available on amazon.com

Author inquiries and mail orders:
Finishing Line Press
PO Box 1626
Georgetown, Kentucky 40324
USA

Table of Contents

All That Is Solid Melts

Into Thick Air 2

Three 3

This Face 5

Five months before Mando died 7

Breathe 8

Passages: in Peru

Water in an Eye 11

Sidewalk Pieces 13

Small Boxes 15

The Hole in the Hill: El Hueco de la Huaca 17

Memory, Aspirated

Marrow Donor 20

Hand Grenade 21

What happened to his body 23

Tilesetter 24

Lost 25

Twelve days 27

Where Would You Have Gone, Young Reporter?

Into What Danger 29

You, the Listener 30

Hurt Inhaled 31

Story, Vanished 32

In memoriam
Armando Alters Montaño 1989-2012

All That Is Solid Melts

Into Thick Air

Stark upright
bolt-clear awake
        1:20 a.m.

Something wrong
Some terrible wrong

Window open to the dense air:
A whoosh—as if the universe
has sucked oxygen
        and with it, substance.

Hours later, word
        of what happened
jackknifes my body
        belly burning
        breath stolen
        light scattered—

All that is solid
        melts
into a hole
in the air.

Three

1.

The doctor scowls
and slaps the air
toward clinical photographs
of a body unclothed,
skin glazed in raw light.

*You have failed
to identify him,* she says.

No, it's him, I say, a beat too late
for the lab-coated head of the morgue
as Marjorie, his editor,
hovers next to me
on this night
of the Mexican elections
he would have covered.

Marjorie translates the Spanish
I should have understood.
Doubt, expanded.
The photos have nothing
to do with my son.

2.

Glass window
Steel table
Body: naked

   long legs stretched out
   hole in one calf
   shape of limbs still perfect

3.

Steel stretcher on asphalt
behind a van, motor idling.
His lips are pulled back,
teeth bared
like a skeleton's,
flesh turned to wax,
to plasticine.

I touch what was him
and hear a scream.
Mine.
The driver shouts.
Marjorie's arm goes across
my shoulder.

We have shuttled
from morgue
to police station
and back, obliged
to identify the body
three times.

It's him, I say.

Marjorie presses.
She's there.
It's him.

But it is not.

Brown hair falls
over his forehead
as always
but even that
looks abandoned.

This Face

You sit in a glass-walled office
at the morgue in Mexico City,
studying a cadaver photograph
of a face you love. You are trying
to convince the coroner
you know this face,
this young man who was smiling
the last time you saw him.
In your face she has glimpsed
a blankness, a momentary
refusal to acknowledge
that the photograph depicts
your son. You barely understand
it reveals the what, not the why,
of random murder.

You have on your phone
another photograph of your son
from three months earlier. He's looking
over his right shoulder into the camera,
smile stretched the width of his face,
underlining cheekbones just before a burst
of laughter as he shows his father
his favorite place: the Newseum,
where typewriters, Teletypes,
Linotypes and laptops are all the same
to him—a way to tell stories. It's where
he goes to think,
to explain hard things, to keep,
as he says, his integrity as a journalist.
The Newseum is where
he will say his vows
with a man he has yet to meet—
he is sure of future love.

He is twenty-two.

His father's camera has caught
the lift of his chin, ready
for his new job as a reporter,
new city, Mexico. In a walk home
one night, perhaps he failed
to see danger.

You are left
with this:
a photograph transfigured
into a sacred relic,
a shard of memory,
story untold.

Five months before Mando died

Trayvon Martin was killed
as he walked home.
This could happen to Mando,
Mario said.
We watch his parents,
resolute and sad,
on a hotel television
afterwards
as we travel
in a grief stupor.

Breathe

Cold doesn't penetrate
sun surfaces
mid-walk

breath scrapes
the valley of my wool scarf.

   Is he really dead?

*

In a city in Mexico years ago,
a stray dog trotted ahead
brown fur pulled
over bulldog skull,
no spare meat
on hard bone,
claws rasping
pocked asphalt.

It was midnight,
not safe, some said, but the dog
took me a good mile to my door
scent of fresh corn
and diesel
lingering around us.

*

At daybreak
a light wind
time layers—

Memory
aspirated:

> *It's okay, you love me*
> *you'll figure it out*
> *here*
> *in this air.*

Passages: In Peru

Water in an Eye

Vallejo gave me
an almost indecipherable word: *empozarse*,
a verb that puts water in an eye
and leaves it just under the rim
so no one has to say what eye water
becomes when it spills over lash and cheek—
it wells up, quiet
like a reservoir back of a dam
poised to inundate entire canyons,
ancient civilizations,
whole lives. A poet told me
North Americans shouldn't write tears
into a poem because that's mawkish
and even in Latin America
only Neruda could get away with it—well,
actually, Vallejo got away with it even
more deftly than Neruda
but in Buenos Aires
where tears are abundant—*una lagrima* is a drop
of espresso in hot milk—I can't find a tear
in new Argentine poetry,
so when a busybody down the street
wondered why I would leave home
to study Spanish
instead of buying an app to translate
on the spot—who needs
more than English really—
I couldn't explain
the truth is I don't know
why I've forced my brain to butt
against cinderblocks of verbs
and tiny lice-like words that inch
into unexpected places
where even the regular veers
irregular late at night

when no one has the energy
to decipher my gameboy Spanish
including me—so I might have missed the tears
because I read Spanish so slowly, well enough
to slam translators but not nearly sufficient
to describe all I need
at the grocery store which a first grader
holding Mama's hand can do—my son could do that
he could write the hell out of Spanish,
carve jokes with it, drink on it,
and still go strong at 1 a.m. except for that one last
early morning when Spanish was likely
the last human sound he ever heard.
Empozarse means to form pools
which means eye on the verge of spilling water
which means to Vallejo a whole life fits
into that eye and pools form—
but even there he doesn't write tears,
not in that poem.

Sidewalk Pieces

A bulldog rides a skateboard smiling
as the sun sinks into a skein
of dried-out air on the pastel horizon.

She glides among the many Mandos
who shimmer in pedazos in the pink light:
That hair, those lips, the straight-up spine, the eyes.

Engulfed by friends, laughing,
Mando returns my stare,
puzzled, breath suspended.

Ahead on the marigolded sidewalk
he straightens his shoulders,
hastens away, scattering light.

On a slatted bench he listens
thickly, hand on a young man's knee,
holding his breath to stave off tears.

In a plaza cafe he slurps
plain spaghetti, sweetly defiant
in a Bart Simpson t-shirt.

He rises to greet an aged auntie,
charms her with tales of matter
she cannot see.

The next day, no bulldog,
no Mando, not even pieces
in the layers of time-stamped air.

Only a black and gray chessboard
walkway, Alice's looking-glass path
on the wind-wracked cliff, now fogbound.

In a bookstore nearby, a clerk hands me
Los Heraldos Negros open to his favorite poem
about the brother who died so young.

The last two lines:
Miguel, will you hurry
and show yourself? Mama will only worry.

Small Boxes

> *"There are blows in life, so powerful... I don't know!"*
> from *"The Black Heralds"* by César Vallejo

"Do you know how it happened?"
the young curator asks in Spanish
about the execution of Túpac Amaru II,
more than two centuries dead.

"*Tortura,*" I say, not knowing
the words for "drawn and quartered."

In front of us a painting
seared on gray canvas: a black circle
with red inside, fixed
atop a thick black rectangle.

The curator points to four black dots shimmering
outside the rectangle, one for each Spanish horse
that pulled the ropes that stretched
the young revolutionary,
a descendant of the last Inca,
to his death.

We move to another canvas
with four archangels masquerading as pop stars,
three revolutionaries clad in bishop's garb,
and a photo strip of young men, *desaparecidos*,
vanished not so long ago in the *manchay tiempo*,
the time of fear.

She hands me a small black box
provided for each viewer.
Into it I insert my own son's name
on a thin strip of white paper:
"*Con amor: Recuerdo mi hijo,
Armando Alters Montaño,
1989-2012.*"

For the young woman,
I summon up the Spanish
for where he died
and a dissertation
on what I do not know:
la calle desierta,
no sé,
sin sonido,
the Spanish coming
more clearly as the story
becomes more uncertain.
She stares at my dry eyes.
Yo no sé, mi amor,

I don't know.

The Hole in the Hill: El Hueco de La Huaca

She lives next to a hole,
I thought she said,
an archeological dig
that dominates her neighborhood,
where someone uncovered
bones of children who were killed
to slave for the rich in the afterlife,
bones of women who were rulers
and sacrificial offerings—
a civilization encased in dirt.

I want to see this, to find out
how someone digs for answers
when people die.

All morning I walk past jacarandas
and corrugated fences
until the sidewalk dead-ends
and a steep hill towers
above the houses.
On terraces hacked
into the hillside
stand bookshelves
laden with books.

Edging closer, I see
no library—
only earthen rectangles
holding adobe bricks
stacked upright like books.
Air accumulated
in the spaces in between
has shored up the hill,
kept it solid
for fifteen centuries.

At the crest of the upturned hole,
where the ocean and the Andes
shimmer through light and dust,
I have dredged no answers
beyond my own confusion.
As air gathers around phantom texts,
I begin the descent
toward home.

Memory, Aspirated

Marrow Donor

Three years after his bones
burned to ashes
they come looking for the marrow.
A child needs a transplant.

His, a match. The voice,
innocent. A call from my son
will right the world.

Why he offered
a piece of himself
so vital to his being,
I don't know.

In a gray rain,
boxed in my car
at an expired meter,
I suppress a ghostly panic:
he could not have known
how much it hurts
to pull tissue
from live bone.

I am so sorry,
the marrow seeker says.
*I am proud
he wanted to help*, I say,
throat thick with sorry.

Hand Grenade

I lob your name
like the tiniest hand grenade,
having paused
for only a microsecond
to think: Is this a good idea
with friends for whom your absence
is not the central point of their existence?

Five of us are painting
Tessa's walls on a hot summer day
when somebody begins to sing
99 Red Balloons.

Mando liked that too, I say
as brushes stop
paint congeals
and sweat drops halt their slow roll
down grimy surfaces of skin.

*He had the most eclectic taste
in music*, Tessa offers,
More than anyone I know,
she says as all eyes rivet
to the work in front of us.

It is a kindness,
her slowing the trajectory
of the little bomb
to spare me
the full impact of its landing.

I do not babble on
about the CD I kept
in my car for two years
until it started to skip—
"Mando/New Coast Camera Club"
it says, in your handwriting.
It is definitely eclectic:
> *David Bowie*
> *Santigold*
> *New Order*
> *a peppy song in Portuguese*
> *an indistinct ballad*
> *a chorus with the phrase "some men die in a fall."*

Some things are better left
to psychic sweat,
veins of imaginary color
an ever-roving inner eye.

Your name a summons
a flash of story
a hope that someone
will match my song
with another as if
they already have you
in their own bandolier
of irrepressible weapons.

What happened to his body

Lezley McSpadden insists
we follow the police bullets
through her son Michael Brown.
Nobody had to live
the way I have to live,
she shouts, perfectly turning the verb
from *had* to *have*,
bringing history to bear on her grief.

Tilesetter

He likes the tile that reverses
the bird, says he'll use
it as a spirit tile,
a reminder only God is perfect—
humans have the flaws.

I pick up the thread,
tell him about a cottony
young eagle feather that floated
to Roberto and LaVerne
from a cloth unfolded
on a prayer bowl
as they danced to guide my son
safely to the spirit world.

The eagle flies
higher than any other bird—
a good sign,
a shiver in light.

If you ever need a son, I'm here,
he says. He stands in the doorway
where he has paused
to check for dampness
around the shower pan. His revolver
is on his right hip.

I will call you every Mother's Day,
he says.

Lost

I lost a scarf
the other day.

Thrift-store cheer—
    yellow there,
        purple here,
    red sails
        blue sky
            black hull
    an abstract boat.

It must have
slipped away
when I walked
the city,
    distracted.

The first time I wore it
my son admired
the way its colors
    lit up my eyes,
the way its cotton
    took the dye.

    I thought
when I lost him

I would never
mourn
another loss.
    All would
    pale.

But absence
lingers
in its own space
      clings
to my neck.

To this
        I acquiesce.

Twelve days

after Mando's first birthday
in his absence, twenty children
and six adults
died, shot
at their elementary school.
We watch the memorial,
gripped by a small boy
who looks like Mando
as he sings a prayer
and a Methodist woman
who looks like my mother.
She wears a scarf
imprinted with images
of every face.

Where Would You Have Gone, Young Reporter?

Into What Danger

Liberia, Sierra Leone, Guinea?
Ebola the virus | ebola the fear | ebola the bodies
    in trenches, bags,
        under the family quilt.

Syria, Morocco, Sudan?
Bullet over there | hand grenade here | a Kalashnikov cradled
    in a dead man's arms.

Spain, France, Portugal?
Death and memory | medieval colonies for modern times |
    a bomb at Atocha station.

Would you have been collateral damage |
journalist imprisoned | object lesson |
    terms of confinement negotiated:

solitary or communal | concrete or dirt |
Bible or Koran slammed in the toilet |
    food tube up the ass or down the throat?

You, the Listener

Would you have followed Bourdieu into a banlieue
down paint-peeled hallways to humans disparaged |
    skin loathed?

You, so willing to hear.
We had life-changing talks in every doorway, Max said.
    A story for every story.

You, with your disarray of dark curls,
face so mutable cab drivers never guess your origins:
    French? Argentine? Israeli?

You they would interrogate first: What are you |
where are you from | why are you here | please hear our stories
    O God O Allah O Nuestra Señora.

Hurt Inhaled

You called me from the Golden Corral, a coffee shop
on the Tohono O'odham nation.
    Mom, he cried, you said.

In the middle of a story about his boyhood hunt in the desert,
a man cried. No more jackrabbits | deer | javelina
    only dung-colored copper-mine slag.

What should I have done? You listened well, I said.
My praise for you, a student. I had faith
    The New York Times

would help you sort out how it hurt
from the story in your notebook.
    In this, we were innocent.

If I still had faith, would I be pain-free?
    Unholy? The mother—
    breath steady, still worried?

Story, Vanished

Would you have returned to Buenos Aires, strolled
past the old death house a few doors down
      from the family you stayed with

who were busy raising children, noticed nothing,
no *detenidos* | no *desaparecidos*
      on their greenclad *avenida*?

History remembered lightly; two fathers in transglobal argument:
      You Mexicans always talk history.
      But at least we Mexicans have a history.

Would you have remained in Mexico, the known,
the incomprehensible: La Condesa all hip and airy
      French expats | Mexican *popis* | common thieves?

It took us four days, only days, to bring your ashes
across the border in a small shiny wooden box | golden crucifix
      your hybrid name on a tiny brass plate.

Additional Acknowledgments and Notes

Many have made this chapbook possible. Thank you to poets Elizabeth Robinson, Edward Hirsch, Andrea Rexilius and the late Chris Ransick, who all understood what I was trying to do before I did. Gratitude to Gail benEzra, Lois Levinson, Kirsten Morgan, Harriet Stratton, Erika Walker and Connie Zumpf, members of the writing group we formed at our literary home, the Lighthouse Writers Workshop in Denver. To friends who guided my Spanish in three countries, mil gracias. I am grateful to Mark Doty, Jericho Brown and Ross Gay for their kindness in intense workshops. To family and friends, including close friends of Mando's who became mine, you have sustained me in countless ways. Your photos, paintings, essays, visits, random texts, letters and memories of Mando show me the power of our family of humans. To Grinnell College English professors Dean Bakopoulos and Ralph Savarese, whose teaching and writing inspired Mando, thank you for also befriending and inspiring me, and dedicating an annual Writers@Grinnell lecture to him. Thank you to Dale Maharidge, Michael Williamson, Stephen Kuusisto, Wil Haygood, Hanif Abdurraqib and Jean Guerrero for delivering the Mando lectures. To Tessa Cheek, Tricia Waters, Vicki Burrichter, Barbara Johnstone, Marilyn Banuelos, John Lawson and Bebe Santa-Wood, thank you. To faculty and students at the New York Times Student Journalism Institute, thank you for showing me, every year, the energy and dedication of young journalists. To Mando's colleagues and mentors at the Associated Press bureau in Mexico City, a simple thank you will never be enough. And finally to Mario Montaño: Without your love, I could not have done this.

Royalties from the sale of this chapbook will go to the Armando Alters Montaño '12 Writers@Grinnell Endowment Fund at Grinnell College.

Diane Alters is a former journalist and college professor who turned to poetry when her son died in 2012. She studied poetry at the Lighthouse Writers Workshop in Denver. Her poems have appeared in *Calyx, Crosswinds Poetry Journal, The New York Quarterly* and *Pilgrimage Magazine*, among others.

www.ingramcontent.com/pod-product-compliance
Lightning Source LLC
LaVergne TN
LVHW041552070426
835507LV00011B/1055